LEAKED FOOTAGES

African POETRY BOOK SERIES

Series editor: Kwame Dawes

LEAKED FOOTAGES

Abu Bakr Sadiq

Foreword by Kwame Dawes

University of Nebraska Press / Lincoln

The African Poetry Book Series is operated by the African Poetry Book Fund. The APBF was established in 2012 with initial support from philanthropists Laura and Robert F. X. Sillerman. The founding director of the African Poetry Book Fund is Kwame Dawes, Holmes University Professor and Glenna Luschei Editor of *Prairie Schooner*.

Acknowledgments for the use of copyrighted material appear on pages 75–76, which constitute an extension of the copyright page.

The University of Nebraska Press is part of a land-grant institution with campuses and programs on the past, present, and future homelands of the Pawnee, Ponca, Otoe-Missouria, Omaha, Dakota, Lakota, Kaw, Cheyenne, and Arapaho Peoples, as well as those of the relocated Ho-Chunk, Sac and Fox, and Iowa Peoples.

♾

Library of Congress Control Number: 2024941785

Set in Garamond Premier.

for Aisha, my mother, who i pray
Jannah Firdaus is written for
for Jafar

Drowning people
Sometimes die
Fighting their rescuers
—OCTAVIA E. BUTLER

People see what they want to see.
And, in most cases, what they are told to see.
—ERIN MORGENSTERN

CONTENTS

FOREWORD

KWAME DAWES

back in their now almost roofless house, a girl
ask her mother if they've reached the point
in their suffering where they can say they've
survived
—"REACHING AN END POINT"

At some point there has to be a reckoning with the way in which our lives
are inundated with the clipped images of terrible violence and suffering from
all around the world that arrive through the ubiquitous persistence of social
media. The stories come without context, without the promise of accuracy, but
the images accumulate into a series of interruptions of our lives—destruction,
blood, suffering, and much more. And at times these images are local yet seem
as if they exist in another continent, and those in another continent come
to us as intimacies. The reckoning is coming in poems, in the ways in which
poets must find language for this peculiar emotional trauma, this assault that
is strangely soothing for its normalizing, and acutely haunting for its persis-
tence in connecting with our day-to-day traumas. There is no question of the
real and the unreal. Abu Bakr Sadiq knows so much and knows so little, feels
so much and feels so little. Yet, there are moments when Sadiq seems to have
begun to engage this "other country" and its dialect and its rules as being in
need of a language to translate it into meaning. *Leaked Footages* is formed by

Sadiq's effort to use what he knows of poetry to chronicle the peculiar world of deeply personal biographies and the emerging biographies shaped by the algorithms of attendant parallel existence and world.

It has been impossible to read the poems in *Leaked Footages* without struggling with their powerful prophetic quality—not in their capacity to predict the future—not in that sense—but in the manner of the ancient prophets whose tasks it is to bring a divine truth to bear on the reality of our daily lives, the things we are doing to ourselves in this historical moment. When poetry, no matter when written, has a capacity to seem urgent and current and aware, it is doing something that is hard to predict or even to achieve except by being present with language and sentiment in the moment. This is why, on November 17, 2023, I read these lines and think that there is something deeply urgent and disarming about the way it captures the horrors of the moment—the horrors in Gaza. It does not matter that the poet may not have had Gaza in mind, though it is clear that they have always had the historical moment that has brought us to Palestine at this time in mind. So that when the poet says "God's silence" the poet has entered something even more startling, something at the heart of our human incapacity to comprehend what we are doing to each other.

One must, however, speak of what is so impressive about this poet—his capacity to see the world and then extract from it the thing that will resonate, the detail that transforms the way we encounter what seems ordinary and normal. In "Rhubarb Shot," Sadiq describes the missing girl, and the way that she is described heightens the terrible loss of her. Yet it is in that final image— the final line of the stanza—that we arrive at the poetic genius—the thing that makes the poet necessary:

> while buildings topple at the center of the city
> on a radio show, a woman calls in to report
> a missing daughter. left home for school at seven.
> last seen on a school bus. fourteen. light skinned.
> hair covered in hijab. skirt, large enough
> to fit two girls her size. has memorized
> the Qur'an. fluent in hausa & pidgin & arabic

& english. speaks like her lineage
lives on her tongue. smells of seawater.

"smells of seawater." "smells of seawater." The detail is elusive and yet precise—
she is a child of travel, a child of salt places, a child of journeying, a child
cleansed by the most natural force in the world—she smells of the sea, and she
is lost, taken, or worse, and so her loss evokes the salt of tears, the lamentation
of seawater.

The poet takes us deeply into a world in which news, information, intimacy,
and the shaping of our sense of the world are being conducted through tiny
screens (video games, YouTube, Instagram, Facebook, streaming films and
videos, etc.), and they are no less visceral and defining for being the product
of a cyber world—a world in which information proliferates without clarity
or easy management. The troubled questions that arise are eloquently offered
in these poems. Here the poet is caught between a sense of faithful devotion
and the troubling reality of violence:

i whisper the word *brother* & my throat asks me for every drop of water in our
bloodied rivers. at a party, a boy sings to me about bullets & blood. his voice,

heavy with the echoes of gunshots & i wonder, if there are angels
singing songs like this in heaven for all the people i've lost.

In the poem "Apocalypse" the poet enters that inevitable place of almost
blasphemy, which is as sacred an expression of faith or the desperate desire
for faith that there is, and in language that combines the banal with the sub-
lime, we reenter the proverbial dark night of the soul. It is a rite of passage,
familiar, and yet necessarily intimate and refreshingly personal as the best
poems ought to be:

i'd convinced my friends i was an alien on a brief visit to planet earth
    where everything
burned; especially places where faithful believers named the houses of
    God. by the time

the apocalypse began, i wondered if God was now homeless & if I could
   invite Him
over for dinner sometime. before the apocalypse began, my people
   worshipped gods

molded out of clay. wept when their prayers fermented in their mouths,
   unanswered.
by the time the apocalypse began, i was convinced God lived everywhere.

And then in "Mutilation Theory" we are faced with a poem that captures
the trauma of being intimately connected to violence and the news of violence:

it   i have images of   my hometown
before it got cropped out of the city
sometimes   i get bored of counting how many
people have gone missing   how many children
have been orphaned   how many are
walking barefoot on the streets   with a family
photograph in their hands   how many are in
prison cells crawling back   in memory to open
windows to a peaceful world   buried in their
                              past

Here we have a framework for the way that trauma arrives and how Sadiq
cannot deny himself from the wounding that happens. In "Video Village," we
are met with the world of images, videos, and inhuman and wholly human
accounting of the lives being lived. The poet finds the poetry in clips and
memes, which are best rendered in a poetic form that finds its force in the
circularity of images turning around in loops and loops:

gunshots, spread over the city's silence. i knew why
my prayers sounded like threnodies echoing in hallways.
i fell, like a wingless bird, on my knees, as i listened to
a woman in a refugee camp weave her hometown

on the hemless fabric of everything she has lost to mutiny.
a prayer fell off my lips when i heard her say
her lost ones live in her dreams. in a room full of tv sets,
on the first screen, i see a sullen-eyed woman in hijab.

These are poems that chronicle the cost of war, the cost of passion, the cost of political delusion, the cost especially on family and on the many minds that must contend with it. In one of the most moving poems in the collection, "Homecoming," the poet addresses a person dear to them about the ways in which these larger matters of geopolitical disruption create deeply wounded victims—the women, the families, the children:

that you do not remember picking up the phone
to be told that your father has forgotten his way
back home again. that he's probably out there
naked, shooting at imaginary enemies in a war
that has been over for over a hundred years—
before colonization, national flags & anthems.
it must mean a lot to the world
that i am holding you in my arms, & you are not
trailing off into the dark corners of another memory.
that my hands reach for yours & i am not met
with blood. that on the floor where we lay,
our bodies, simmering in sweat, i read to you
about birds & flight, to keep them both alive
you let a sky unfold from the alleys of your palms
for the first time in years since he left you & your
mother, to fight out of love for his country;
since he returned with the silencer of a 9mm pistol
dangling like a cigar, from his mouth; with stories where
every character dies with a bullet between their eyes
& he, the teller, blames it on the quiet of his audience.

The poet's sense of place and the evocation of the geopolitical space and landscape of Nigeria is one of the striking things about the collection. The names of places like Borno, Lagos and Dar es salaam, Minna, and Maiduguri achieve a ritualistic power of naming that threads the collection.

The poet's facility with idiom and voice registers is one of the most promising things about this collection because of what it signals for the future. His shifting registers do not seem like the gesture of an emerging poet desperate to show all that they can do but arise in response to the demands of the poem. In the poem "After a Conversation with Janazah with S in a Dream," the profane language reveals a raw vulnerability—at once sacrilegious and at the same time an expression of frustration and earnestness:

> but man, these things kinda look so much like me. but we are fucking
> good,
> right? I mean, if I keep my head down, go on about writing poetry on the
> leaflets
>
> of my sedatives & nurse every bruise I pick from falls while sleepwalking
> out of my nightmares, right? I must say though, my God, fuck these
> nightmares.

There is an American mockery here, a canned pseudo-American accent with idioms like "keep my head down" and "kinda look so much like me," but the couplet that follows lays out with raw language the anxieties around their mental condition—the sedatives, the sleepwalking, the nightmares. Sadiq is aware of these different registers, aware of the terrain that he is venturing into, and aware that what is affected here is an emotion that is arresting and moving.

This collection could have been called "The Cyborg and Me" given the number of poems that include the "Cyborg." The cyborg is never defined. It is introduced as if the audience must know who or what this "cyborg" is. It is a term that has grown out of the science fiction reel of books, comics, films, and television, but that has settled into the complex world of the video game. To the poet, the cyborg is the final enacted contemporary humanity—the merging of the robot with the organic human being, and in Nigeria the cyborg is at home, a kind of familiar monster and alter ego for the poet—one who plays chess with the poet and has coffee with the poet, even as it leads protests and causes violence in the streets of the city. A close study of the cyborg in these poems will yield great reward. In the poem "Uncensored Footage of the Cyborg Leading a Protest in Lagos," the cyborg appears in the city of Lagos as part of a protest. The poet does not find this image remarkable, but for him the cyborg's presence is inextricably connected to violence. The collection does not end with a quality of hopelessness or a succumbing to the end of human kindness, and this may perhaps be the point of the collection at one level. But the haunting presence of the cyborg is impossible to ignore:

the crowd chants

for freedom; for a day, faithful enough to let love blossom. in the video,
the cyborg is seen seething through scrums of bullets. there's a version

that ends where the cyborg feeds death to its own end & elsewhere,
a woman sings the national anthem before burning our country's flag.

Abu Bakr Sadiq has, by dint of this striking collection, launched a career that holds tremendous promise and challenge. We can take comfort in the power of poetry to teach us the language we need to contend with and understand the changes taking place in our world, the advances in technology, the shrinking of the globe, the destruction of the environment, and the manner in which our sense of nation and identity is in deep and inevitable flux. Sadiq manages to offer us ways to engage with these changes in language that are compelling, beautiful, and extremely resourceful.

ACKNOWLEDGMENTS

Immense gratitude to my family, whose unwavering love, support, and patience with me while I worked on this collection will continue to astound me 'til eternity: Musa Ibrahim, Hafsat, Zulai, Nuhu, Sakinat, Jafar, Adam, Hassan, Ramatu, Ruqayya, Ahmed Tanimu, Fatimah. Thank you B. M. Dzukogi, Aremu Adams Adebisi, Nome Emeka Patrick, Alycia Pirmohamed, Saddiq Dzukogi, Olumide Fayomi, Chukka Lotanna Thomas, for the gift of your words and guidance.

With deep admiration, I am grateful to these people, without whose indelible wisdom, love, and courage this work would have been too daunting to do: Martins Deep and Mayowa Oyewale, your eyes are my gifts from God. Thank you Sihle Ntuli, Younglan Talyoung, Ibrahim Babátúdé Ibrahim, Aishat Adesanya, Hindatu Usman, Ramadan Abubakar Deze, Paul Salasi Gwammache, Michael "Rage" Imona, Maryam Usman, Maryam Abdulkadir Yerima, Peter Kwange, Michael Godwin Odeh, Rofi'ah Akinyemi Adedolapo, Sufyaan Yakubu, Shamsiyya Yusuf Gambo, Mustapha Balarabe, Zainab Kuyizhi, Zainab Ilyasu Bobi, Ernest Chibuzor Ani, Nwuguru Chidiebere Sullivan, Sodïq Onyèkànmí, Samuel Samba, S. A. Ibrahim, Faruk Alfe, Ismail Faruk Muhammad, Muazu Ahmed Shuaib, Paul Chuks, Jakky Bankong-Obi, and everyone whose hand I've held through this journey.

Thank you to my second family, the Deadliners: Anthony Okpunor, Roseline Mgbodichinma Anya-Okorie, Samuel A. Adeyemi, Praise Osawaru,

Anointing Obuh, Semilore Kilaso, Abdulbasit Yusuff, Kei Vough Korede, Ameen Animashaun, Timi Sanni, Elizabeth Ejiro Edward, Rahma Oluware-milekun Jimoh, Chiwenite Onyekwelu, Dipe Jola, Elias Udo-Ochi, Timothy Ojo, Ruona Idjenughwa, the light of your souls illuminates my world. Many, many thanks to Hilltop Creative Arts Foundation, Artmosterrific Residency, Ishola Abdulwasiu, Flight School Workshop, Tampered Press, Koleka Patuma, and Ladan Osman.

LEAKED FOOTAGES

Introducing Bhabi to the Cyborg

just so we're clear, you're not allowed to ask
how these scars came to be.
i don't usually respond to questions
concerning lineage. i did not choose
to wake up & find my family gone.
unlike you, i am not more machine than
human. i exist in multiple halves. half water.
half wind. half gunsmoke. half eulogy.
half rage. half homeless. half patriotic.
half burnt. i am never who i say i am.
i am good at telling lies. this too is a lie.
once, a few gunmen invaded our villages.
dragged women & girls by their hijabs
into a skyless forest. we are done trying
to get used to being ushered
into the morning light
by incessant gunfire. to witness the night
here is to open yourself to the nudity
of bloodshed. when asked by a stranger
about how many people i've lost, i began
with my name & the dead still haven't
stopped leaking through my mouth.
it's better if you never ask the locals
how to dress a country's wound
that wouldn't stop bleeding.
i know of widowed women whose hands
have held ash from burnt bodies. it's likely

we may never meet again. i am the type
to thirst for sleep in the middle of a world
tumbling towards its end. please,
remember me that way.

WORMHOLE

the way the days are peeling away now
is the same way they did before we got here.
yesterday, i bumped into a drone at a festival.
its face, a telegram from my great grandfather.
& because there's a synchronous touch to events,
the moments come to us unseparated.
in this one, as his mother's only son
my great grandfather is still being born
in the same hospital my father would later meet
my mother in. at the same time, my mother
has just given birth to me. she takes a picture
with her phone & sends it to my father,
who is worlds away from home.
& somewhere still,
the invention of the first mobile phone
is being debated upon. time dissolves
& we are a billion light-years deep
into the future. i speak & my voice travels
faster than light. i speak & a drone floats
on the spine of my words. through time travel,
we wrap memories around our fingertips. in one,
i am sitting on a bench, watching my father
kneel to propose to my mother in the same garden
she would later die in. & at the same time,
i am waving my grandfather goodbye
at the shore of the mediterranean sea.
at the same time, we never get to the shore
because the ship never arrives. time telescopes

& my mother is still alive, taking a flying car
to harvest water from clouds. & at the same time,
we feed the sky to climate change. time telescopes,
the future mirrors the past. the present, a gold coin
rotting in our palms. & at the same time,
i am riding a fire-breathing unicorn to a janazah.
we pour dragon milk into paper cups
& toast to the uselessness of time. excuse me.
i'm sorry. i think i missed something. i mean,
Bhabi, what year is it again?

ROAD MAP

i was born at the end of summer. then,
i knew nothing
about loss. i think a lot about life
underwater. i desire the wrong things. wrongs things being
cities, peaceful enough for me to call home. home being
where i never have to worry about watching
everything i love disappear into the dark alleys
of death. i make memories up to remind myself of a life
i never had. before uni, i lost my mother & so my softness
was born. i know i'm not the only motherless boy in this city.
i got my name from my grandfather—alphabets, scrambled
to translate into "crocodile" in my mother tongue.
which explains my undying love for water & how it never
passes through anywhere unnoticed. some days, it's impossible
getting sleep. on others, i tell myself my spirit animal
is a koala. i wish i could fill the bones of this city
with enough tenderness to break its chain of suffering.
my idea of home moves
like a river. what i fail to forget, i name after an ancestor
i never met. i sleep thinking about what a burnt body
would say if its ashes grew a mouth.
i have a phobia for leaving anywhere
that makes my body feel at home. at 12, i believed
i knew everything it meant to be lost until
i was asked where i'd go if i were to search for myself.

MAQTOOB

i mumble duas against my desires for what's gone. a sheikh at the masjid
tells me to accept my losses with faith. says everything had been written

long before i came into existence. the fate of brother's broken tooth
lost in an accident only Allah saw coming. the fate of my right ankle

before i twisted it on a bicycle after school. the fate of my country—
a ray of light, lost beneath the shadow of a night sky. the fate of my heart

beating in unison with the breath of burning cities. the fate of my ears
deafened by jets of gunfire. the fate of the wind blowing through nights

i fill the air in my room with supplications. the fate of my faith
opening its chest to accept the will of Allah. maqtoob. maqtoob. every word

already written. so i should consider why the missing boy's face stays stretched
above my memory. maqtoob. maqtoob. all of my life, an uncovered erasure

of what was written by Allah. so i should consider the end, where every will shall
pass. consider empty playgrounds, aching for the feet of children. consider what

should be a blessing: i have lost so much but not a memory of everything i've lost.

Explaining Bot Fights to Bhabi

to win the fight, your mind has to move
faster than a walking marshmallow.
it is okay to lose a digit or two. or a whole
limb. we've all lost something we thought
we couldn't live without. in my last bout
my bot broke most of the bones of its
titanium skeleton. bled mounds
of electrons into its bedsheets. i feared
it was going to die before sunrise until
it didn't. for nights, i dreamt only of
cyborgs in heaven. nobody knows how
it has survived this long. perhaps,
you & i are not the only ones
with an insatiable hunger
for strips of sunlight. in a battle against
a swarm of microbots, you will have to
assume that you've lost everything
there is to lose. that the future of
everyone you love is crammed in the belly
of your remote controller; that a day
will come when our bodies will lie beside
each other, wondering where the world
will whisk away to in the event where
time softens into an inflatable dinosaur.

anyway, the fight can only be over when
a bot is destroyed. this red button is your
trigger. with your thumb on it, your bot
fights like a wounded beast 'til the other
bot dies. ever imagined, if that's the same
thing that happens when humans fight
each other? you have been asleep for six
months. open your mouth. i'm dying to
kiss your lips again. where is your tongue?

Uncensored Footage of the Cyborg in an IDPS Camp

every city my tongue had taught itself to call home
                                   remains lost
in the endless shaft of my memories   if i speak
about loss   i know exactly which wound i would be waking
while the country crumbles outside my room   i sit on a couch
pressing play   to watch the cyborg walk through the gates
to watch women sitting on verandas   whisper words
into each other's ears   while pointing at the metals
on the cyborg's arms   the evening sun warming their faces
i watch children play tag   untouched by the news
miles away from their fences   of many towns
being limbed by firearms   of bloodied water
flowing into rivers   on the edge of the city
in the footage   the cyborg squats over a soldier's boot
rotting at the feet of a watchtower   some women
in the camp   came from towns where half the houses
have been razed to ashes   others cannot speak
of their families   without bruising the sheen
of their memories   inside a tent   a man with a disfigured
face   offers the cyborg a journey through the ruins
of his past life   where no one knew the dark days
of mourning   looking away from the footage   i stare
at my mother's photograph   separated from its frame

FLIGHT THEORY

it's not my place to question why they left
what more can i say   that my silence hasn't
already given air to   in their shoes   i would
have done the same   even the patriots
at some point   get tired of waking to
smoke-filled cityscapes   i know if i pretend
well enough to be winged   i might live
the rest of my life in the sky   yunno
somewhere God will not have to stretch
to hear my cry   to ask where in my lineage
is bleeding   whose body i'm searching for
in rivers   which city i'd like to go   to pour
my ache away   why every departure opens
a hole in my memory   i understand why
i am scared of leaving   not everyone i've said
goodbye to   made it past the lake chad basin
forty percent of the children are caught up
in the middle of refugee crises   & my lord
i am not done being a child   & my lord
i am still in love   with the buzzing
of airplanes   every night   i go to sleep
thinking about where i can fly to   without
the scars in my stories   telling everyone
                    where i came from

CRANE SHOT

i've heard people say
i'm alive   only because all i've seen of the birth
                             of mutiny has been through the eye
                             of a camera. i, a mouthpiece
without any memory   of what is lost when a home is arched
into a field   of honor. i see it all. but i cannot save
anyone. i cannot
play God. i play it safe
hiding behind the hand
of a crane. my eyes,
glued to camera screens.
even from above,
i can tell   who has lost what & who's waiting for
                             whose return. the women, i know,

have given up hopes
of the return of
their men & now busy
themselves
making up names of   inexistent countries
to tell their children,
when they ask
where their fathers
have gone.   in a rough footage,
                             i see a mother kiss her daughter's
forehead after *salaat al-fajr*.
her eyes, glinting
with choked back tears.   in another,
                             i watch an aerial shot of a central market—

a suicide bomber walks in,
whispering the *shahada*
minutes before pressing
his thumb on a detonator.   in another, pupils are pulled
off a school bus.   in another, i watch
from above,
a funeral procession
for forty corpses   wrapped in white linen. i beg to stretch
the hours of my little
omnipresence. to be a   witness at the end of these erasures.

After Bhabi Dreams of a City Filled with Light

an *āyah* in the Qur'an says Allah has promised
gardens of bliss to all believers. tired, i light
a broken candlestick. its flame, a miniature sun,
spreads to douse the darkness in my room.

thinking of what could happen next in the city,
i grow cold, like a smile, trapped inside a tear duct.
in a mirror, i search my eyes for traces of joy.
i beg Allah to flatten out this knoll of fear growing
in my chest. for long, i've lived like a firefly, arcing
the shadow of a white sky. my mouth, a broken
boombox, replaying moments nursed by women
who have now gone missing.

sometimes i hear the muezzin's voice, shrilling through
a microphone. my heart unfolds like a beam,
slipping out of a dark sky. in a village, widowed
women gather to mourn those they've lost. carving
x-shapes above gravestones. in my room, i imagine my
younger self, zigzagging through these graves,
blind to what lies inside.

zodiacal light spills through my window shutters. even after
years of wading through white rivers of time, in search of
x-ray photographs of my flooded wells of memories,
i still feel like a veiled silhouette, shuddering in the middle
of an empty room. under a white circle of light, drawn by
a lamp, my fingers trace the city's map with the faithfulness
of a smile, loosening itself on a teary face.

in the city, prayers are being offered to stifle
the obliteration of peace from the heart of our
new country as it crawls, blind-eyed, toward an oasis.
i ask Allah, lifting cupped palms in the air, for a home
knotted in a windstorm of serenity; to make me a jailbird,
locked inside the walls of His immeasurable plains of mercy.

close, i hold a mirror to my face, hoping i find memories
of our glorious days, glinting behind the filmy eyes
of history. on the news, a woman ends a report on
abducted girls returning home, drained as bones
emptied of marrows. on my bed, i curl beneath my blanket
anxious as a shadow waiting to be erased by light.

Ars Poetica with a Broken Shahada

it is too late to pray that the next *salaat* my people stand to offer
doesn't turn out to be another *janazah*.

a lot has changed around here. there's no one left to tell exactly
where the city's bright lights disappeared into.

after a quiet walk through an empty neighborhood, Bhabi tells me
that the bloodstains i'd seen, strewn across

the pavements, came from bodies i had shared playgrounds with.
& i know she means my friends

have all outpaced the wind in their lungs; that she might be dead
before i write the next line

in this poem. i confess, there are days when language alone cannot
save you. my people wish to write poems

where they don't have to bury their lovers between metaphors. my
people write poems & pull

blindfolds over lines that remind the world of their beauty. my
people are too tired

of being killed to give two shits about lexicons. on whatsapp,
Ramadan sends me a voice note,

to tell me my people have been hemorrhaging out of their homes.
i watch the video of a boy lying in a pool

of his blood with a bullet between his ribs. his tongue, pushing
the shahada just halfway out of his mouth;

just enough to tell Allah to please pour a rain of sunflowers
over his body, if He can see this.

Report from an Inkblot Test Reveals

i've got a hive of bumblebees for a mind;
i think myself an eyeless shutterbug,
weaving through a maze of memories;
i was raised around women who spoke
with an unquenched thirst for peace;
i dream too much about houses
on fire; my heart feels more like a shattered
window to a roofless room than a jukebox
of psalms; i've been called by many names;
often, an arrow inside a bow, waiting
to be launched; sometimes a serpent,
treading the architectures of bloodied
riverbeds; i've mourned the death of lives
i've only seen on news; i am not the one
to drink from a river, beaten by the bodies
of my dead people; i want to be forgiven
for remembering the faces everyone else
has fought to forget in their sleep; part of me
believes i can make the whole world my home;
another believes i am a beam of white light
lost in a crate of darkness; another believes
i want to love my country even as it turns
a hollow statue trudging the waves of a sea
drowning in its own turbulence.

DISPLACEMENT THEORY

what matters now   is not that even the rivers
are gone   & what's left are twined trails
of white sand   i always knew it would come
to this   it follows a natural course   when
too many lives cling to the same prayer   in the fight
to remain rooted   in their home   someone
has to leave   eventually   abandoned houses
become homes   to the ghosts of those who couldn't
make it across the border   the nights
open themselves to more darkness   some of
the people i love are living a new life
within the walls of refugee camps in dar es salaam
others are busy   undoing the threads of trauma
on the streets of yaounde   i know i should have
chosen to live   like an armless shadow
bleached against a wall   it is easier that way
at least   i wouldn't have to remember much
of the past   or what i've lost   i get to escape
the cruel hands of memory   unscathed   i learn
to draw maps on seashores   with a knife's tip
i get to walk through the neighborhood   offering
salaam to everyone   pretending they're still here

The BBC Explains the Country's Challenges to the Cyborg in Sixty Seconds

after agreeing that so much has gone wrong,
the cyborg & i bend our bodies in *sujood*.
yesterday, we prayed against becoming victims
to the violence of geography. we woke

longing to heal without yielding
to the darkness of exit wounds. i wish i knew
what my heart is most scared of. maybe it is
the men who walk through the eye of the sun

with rifles tucked under their arms.
who i can't promise i know by their names.
only that in islam, i am taught to accept them
as my brothers. i am listening to the cyborg

complain about the country's economy.
i drag my left pinkie through tiny pyramids of dust
on a table. a woman on tv is saying she lost
her children during a retaliatory attack by unknown

gunmen. everything the reporters are telling the cyborg,
i've snitched about to Allah before, in a prayer.
the cyborg thinks there are too many holes
in my mouth. asks why the media is never exact about

body counts. why there are empty villages surrounded
by bloodish-red water. where the girls are taken to after

abduction. do they return whole when they're released.
how many families i've lost to the crisis. how deep has

the trauma clawed into my body. if i think the silicon plate
in his chest can repel bullets, in case they start shooting.
if i would like to go somewhere i can sleep & not be
woken by the sound of rounds, rushing out of firearms.

in response, i ask if he can just shut the fuck up.

RHUBARB SHOT

while buildings topple at the center of the city
on a radio show, a woman calls in to report
a missing daughter. left home for school at seven.
last seen on a school bus. fourteen. light skinned.
hair covered in hijab. skirt, large enough
to fit two girls her size. has memorized
the Qur'an. fluent in hausa & pidgin & arabic
& english. speaks like her lineage
lives on her tongue. smells of seawater.

in the city's center, more buildings are falling.
firefighters continue to pull casualties through
thick smoke. elsewhere, a family is stopped
for security check at the chad border. the father
squeezes naira notes into the palms of the customs
officer. in the backseat, his wife mutters verses
from the Qur'an. from the rearview mirror,
he sees her face, wet with tears.

in the news, they say more buildings might fall &
all residents should evacuate the center of the city.
i watch a woman open her mouth to say a *dua*.
her voice, a string of white noise, echoing
the rumblings of her fears. someplace, students
at a *madrasah* spread prayer rugs on a field.
facing the *qibla*, their eyes fall on roofs brought
down by stormwater, gunfire, & God's silence.

A Patrol Officer Wants to Know

what we've come out to do during curfew hours   if we're aware of what's happening
in the city   why we have pocket-sized copies of the Qur'an with us
what the shahada means   if we can explain in layman's language
if we know anything about the shootings from last night
which one of us plays call of duty best
if our parents know of our whereabouts
what our intentions are with the prayer rugs on our shoulders
if we performed our salaats before leaving home
if we're still in a state of ablution
where we would go in the event of a sudden explosion
if we've lost a family member before
what we would do if we return home to find our parents missing
if we have our IDs with us
if we're true citizens of the country
if we can sing the national anthem
what we think of when we see smoke rising in the city
if we've swam in the river since it got stained by blood
what we'd say to a boy asking where suicide bombers go after death
if we have any relative locked up in prison
if we've participated in a protest before   when was the last time
we slept without hearing the sound of gunshots
how long we think it takes for a bullet wound to heal
we say *bismillah*   open our mouths   & no sound comes after

IN CONVERSATION WITH BHABI

perhaps   when it is all said & done
our mothers will return home
with hands   still as the shadow
of a broken bridge, lying over a river
to tend to the emptiness we've
earned. everything i know about women
from my hometown
remains lost to the blind eye

my memory that has been gone for days
my mother has been gone for days
& we all want to forget the same
things: nights when the ghosts of
burnt cities, claw into our bodies—

we'll find ourselves again
aching to glaze our bodies with the love we've lost
beneath a full moon, shining on the face
our lost ones never saw. everyone wants something
woven, like fabrics, shaped like what my townswomen
whom i have loved before i met
because they look like my mother, whose face
i've longed to love
without

asking everyone why
bhabi's father has been gone for days;
names that reminds us of many
people we loved who chose to become
wounds, widening across our chests

to take the joy Allah is yet to give
to us. the woman i am in love with
tells me now is not the right time
to worry about being in love
she says *home* when i ask where she'd go
if she were to leave our country
once, she told me what we call
our motherland is a graveyard
full of living corpses—
so i return to the Qur'an, to the prayer mat

i prostrate to ask Allah
to drown me in His shoreless rivers
of mercy. i paint an atlas with black ink
making the whole world a single country
for the first time, i pronounce myself
a citizen of the world. i feel a boneless hand
wringing my neck for elegies

so i wish time will bring back my friends & my sister
introduces me to a friend who swears by Allah—
to carry myself through threads of grief where
the body must undo itself from suffering;
to mourn the bloodline of women she'd carry
my sister would fill her mouth with supplications.
nostalgia never dies across borders. i ask if
learning to keep the dead in their graves with prayers
is a way to escape the grips of grief. she doesn't answer
when she sits on the spot our mother died.
i go to Allah
begging Him
for the last time, again, for floods
written for the people of Noah as i try
folding everyone i've lost in a shroud
tonight, both as an angel &
a rotten watchtower's shadow
falling on my mother's grave.

my god swears / by the fig, by the olive, by the brightest star, by the prophet who penned no ghazal

& suddenly, there are more birds in the sky than i can count.
a woman drags a dead cat across a walkway & the streetlights strip into umbras.

all the women in my hometown are good at burying lifeless things:
children & husbands—bulleted in their farms or hosed in a home raid by bandits.

the meat seller swears he knows everything about death because someone he knows
has died every day for two weeks. the thing is, we are mostly good at being alive

until there's more dying to do than living. before dispersing to their houses
a group of men follow each *salaam alaikum* they push off the cliffs of their lips

with a warm stretched arm. in every handshake, i see an invitation to a janazah.
perhaps, being a witness to so much loss scratches away the living animal inside us.

i'm not prophesying when i say by tomorrow, i'll watch my people
gather around a motionless body, quiet as a stone, & fill the air with a chorused

innalillahi wa inna ilayhi raji'un. reminding me, that what i call death is only but
an opening in the back of someone's chest; that i do not need to write

another poem mourning the demise of a brother i never knew by name—
never got to see, before his bones became filled with gunpowder.

on youtube, bearded men with rifles in hand, quote my prophet
to remind me of what he said a muslim is to another muslim.

i whisper the word *brother* & my throat asks me for every drop of water in our
bloodied rivers. at a party, a boy sings to me about bullets & blood. his voice,

heavy with the echoes of gunshots & i wonder, if there are angels
singing songs like this in heaven for all the people i've lost.

Uncensored Footage of the Cyborg at a Shooting Practice

playing on mute / i let the footage loop / over & over
i watch him aim / one eye closed / fire the first shot

through the target's chest / the second / a headshot
pulling my mind back / into the semi darkness / i saw

in the eyes of a shopkeeper / as he laid / with blood
pooling around his face / after a bullet / eased itself

into his jugular vein / pushing Allah / further away
from his soul / too many times / i've witnessed / a shot's

precision precede the arrival of demise / the cyborg aims
at another target / goes for the neck / misses by an inch

my mind shifts / away from the footage / i let my fingers
trace the spine / of my Qur'an / i contemplate / playing

my favorite afro-songs / so loud / the walls wouldn't help
dancing with me / i can pray for peace / all i want / but

i dare not / go anywhere / close to the city / knowing its
heart / is a booby trap / wrapped under / a veil of

unavenged deaths / so i try to forget / the faces of beautiful
women / on tv / announced / to have gone / missing

like the many women / before them / without names
or photographs / where they're not / covered in hijabs

at the end of the footage / i watch the cyborg / walk away
from the camera / with a gun / strapped to his waist

drainAGE

in an IDPs camp, while waiting for my brother's return
i peer through a handful of photographs
taken near a border. some faces, i recognize
from towns no one lives in anymore
behind a van, a soldier presses the burning end
of a cigarette
into a man's chest.
a border patrol
officer glides his hands on the breasts
of two adolescent girls. two men
in tattered trousers lay cuffed by the ankles
to a lamppost. a crowd of children cuddle each other
against the mercy of a cold night; frostbite
flaming across their limbs. across the borders, i learn
neighboring countries are raising red flags
to the faces of refugees. back home, i waste days
tracing in memory, the skeleton of cities i once knew. so many
people have left. some nights, i find myself
in a dream running toward home. only when i reach
the end of the road do i remember there's no one left
to return to.

APOCALYPSE

by the time the apocalypse began, my country was burning behind my back.
my friends & I were speeding on a highway. the music in the car was so loud

we did not hear God calling us by names we'd forgotten our parents gave us.
before the apocalypse, everyone knew Moh' as Muhammad & A.J. as Abduljalal;

Shukuu as Shukrah & Bakari as Abubakar. before the apocalypse, our tongues did
not know to trim Fatima into Teema or to say Mubi when we meant to say Mubarak.

by the time the apocalypse began, we were falling in love with cartoon characters
from Disney; crying when any of them died in an accident that wasn't an accident.

by the time the apocalypse began, our lives were accidents. before the apocalypse began,
i was googling pictures of UFOs captured by NASA. by the time the apocalypse began,

i'd convinced my friends i was an alien on a brief visit to planet earth where everything
burned; especially places where faithful believers named the houses of God. by the time

the apocalypse began, i wondered if God was now homeless & if I could invite Him
over for dinner sometime. before the apocalypse began, my people worshipped gods

molded out of clay. wept when their prayers fermented in their mouths, unanswered.
by the time the apocalypse began, i was convinced God lived everywhere.

MUTILATION THEORY

indulge the ruins   if the truth is what you seek
all you get with me is a mouth   steeped in shame
a mind   filled with
blank memories   whorled in splashes of blood
i am nothing like the skylight   seeping through
holes in brown building tops   i cannot lead you
to where my country's scars began
their journey   i know only of the memory
of what's left   in the ashes of burnt cities
i like me better as a wounded wall   that cannot
remember how many bullets passed
through it   i have images of my hometown
before it got cropped out of the city
sometimes   i get bored of counting how many
people have gone missing   how many children
have been orphaned   how many are
walking barefoot on the streets   with a family
photograph in their hands   how many are in
prison cells crawling back in memory   to open
windows to a peaceful world   buried in their
                                          past

VIDEO VILLAGE

on the first screen, i watch a sullen-eyed woman in hijab
speak of a forgotten lineage, alive only in her memories.
a prayer falls off my lips when i hear her say
her stories are broken souvenirs from the aches she survived.

speaking of a forgotten lineage, kept alive in her memory
a girl wipes her tears with a discolored scarf. i ask if
her stories are broken souvenirs from the aches she survived
before crossing a border, on her way to dar es salaam.

a girl wipes her tears with a discolored scarf. i ask if
anyone has heard of the women who went missing
before crossing a border, on their way to dar es salaam.
a soldier tells me the chaos will stop. i wonder why he says

nobody has heard of the women who went missing
the day i slipped underwater. trying not to be there when
an officer tells me the chaos will stop. i wonder why he said
i should trace maps of burning cities on my atlas.

the day i slipped underwater, trying not to be there when
gunshots spread over the city's silence, i knew why
i should trace maps of burning cities on my atlas.
i fell, like a wingless bird, on my knees, as i listened to

gunshots, spread over the city's silence. i knew why
my prayers sounded like threnodies echoing in hallways.

i fell, like a wingless bird, on my knees, as i listened to
a girl in a refugee camp weave her hometown

on the hemless fabric of everything she has lost to mutiny.
a prayer fell off my lips when i heard her say
her lost ones live in her dreams. in a room full of tv sets,
on the first screen, i see a sullen-eyed woman in a hijab.

6pm at AbdulHameed's Barbershop

what the trash collector does not tell any of
us at the barbershop is that   there's a crowd
gathering around a body by the roadside   &
that the blood on his fingers is   not his own
& that the police would come asking   after
names we'd nailed to our fathers' graves   &
that a woman would hold my leg   on the
street   & ask if i'd seen the man who
killed her son if i'm her son   & that her
face would follow me to bed   & that i
would empty bottles of wine   as always
when i'm helpless   to those who expect me
to know beyond the nothing i know   & that
i would watch many nights   strip to dawns
with my eyes   swirling in their sockets
because i am the god   who carries people's
tragedies & name them his own   i cry
their cries   with their voices breaking in
& out of my throat   & i become them
my heart shrinks like theirs   a wound
grows into an ocean   on their tongues
i fall on my back   into their mouths
& become one with   the salt water
the water forgets   how to drown a boy

like me   i gather what's left of me
into dunes   & go wherever the wind
goes   sometimes all i want is to disappear
& other times i just   want to be here & alive

Everything I've Lost Returns to Me as Wind

it won't be long before the voice
in my voice starts into a song
the song into a memory
of us skyrocketing our hands
into the sand on a beach
to hole up my milk tooth
before the air in my mouth goes dry
before everything i've lost
returns to me as wind
i would open my mouth to say
alhamdulillah
your name would fall like dusk on my lips
you will not be here to put it back
into my mouth & i won't write
to ask if a country reddened at its borders
has fallen out of the wound on your arm
everything i couldn't say to you
i told the wind
silence listens to everything
& what i'm not telling you is that someone
on our street is forgetting the full moon
you had for a face & i'm not the one
& i'm dying with envy watching myself
dissolve into nothingness

i've wanted since learning about your absence
to not write this poem
to not call onto God on the earth you've become
to not try to hide you in metaphors
as empty as the bass in your laughter
to not open myself to destruct like a flesh
opens itself to a bullet like a blade
opens itself into a corpse at an autopsy
but not wanting anything at all in itself is a want

Second Encounter with Bhabi in a Dream

speaking of survival   she tells me she has
no family left in this town but   has made peace
with her loss   her voice an echo chamber   leaking
what's left of the life she's lived   we walk past
an abandoned truck   perforated by bullets
i ask what her days have been like
since the last mass shooting in the central market
sitting on the bank of a bloodred river   she leans
towards my face   my blurred reflection   glistening
in her teary eyes   *emptier* she says
a town i lived in   before it got raided
had drainages   clogged with the ruins of residents
where i loved going out to pick wild flowers
amongst weed growing in uncompleted
buildings   i tell her i once went swimming
& found
the wreck of an armor tank   lying on the riverbed
i hold her hand   as we walk down a street
where half the houses are empty   the owners
either dead   or fled when they could no longer
stand the violence   we stop in front of a car
parked by the roadside   its broken windscreen
jagged like layers of a spider's web   at the end
of the road   we walk back to our rooms
to lie in wait for the arrival of the next ruin

READING BHABI'S DIARY

i find names of all the people she knows
who've fled since the rise of insurgency in
the region. i find unfinished sketches of
women she probably only saw on the news.
in an entry, she speaks of a girl born inside
a refugee camp in dar es salaam. whose
mother left the country after her husband
was shot on his way home from work.
she writes her dreams on the bottom
of each page. in some, she dreams of Allah
taking her away before the country swells
into a glass door tinted by blood. in others,
she mourns the unconfirmed deaths of men
who vowed to love her forever. she writes
in a language that pushes me into the arms
of the silent beauty of white space. i forget
i have stories folded away in the back
of my memory. i read & read & the words
will not stop skidding off my lips.
on the center page, she paints a picture of
a faceless woman with an umbrella, standing
in the middle of a hailstorm. in a different
entry, she writes of mothers, running out of
burning houses with babies strapped to their
backs. her voice, on the page, breaking between
her prayers & the silence that answers them.
on the back page, she writes *my Lord, my Lord,*
listen. take my ache & remake it in your image.

DRIVING DOWNTOWN

the other side breathes quietly   i hear
many people have left   but the town
isn't completely dead   yunno
alive   but in ways that make you think
zombies   think weevil-holed
bean seeds   think half-healed bruises
leaking pints of blood inside a car
i wave back at the woman
in an ice-cream shop   i bop my head
to loud music from barbershops
i drive in silence   asking no one
why half the houses here
are locked   i know all that talk
about inheriting wounds
from bodies you make a home in
i've heard the news—a fingernail
scratching the scars of yesterday's ruins
on the streets   everyone knows how
to run through tear gas   knows
when to keep their names away
from the ache the city lost itself to
i get why everyone asks   which town i came
from   if i know what i'm risking
being on the road   all by myself   if my plans
include returning home before
it gets dark   why i chose to claw
a wound in the middle of healing

Uncensored Footage of the Cyborg
Leading a Protest in Lagos

the only reason guns could ever be fired into a crowd is to witness
the silence a bullet promises. after each shot, time is always the first

to lose its shape. the cyborg tends to think faster than humans at the time
of strife. dumbfounded, an old woman asks what the protest is for.

the cyborg points to her son's stiffened body by the roadside. she weeps.
so much, the tears seep into my bedroom floor. so many stories

have surfaced since the incident. in one, there was never a cyborg
in sight. in another, nobody cared to ask whose face was being

pressed against the asphalt. there would come a time when i would
stop believing in everything my body tells me. a time when i would

stand in the path of a bullet & wait for the cyborg to tell me if i am
still alive or not. a time when i would look through the lens

of a broken periscope & snatch the rifles of policemen aiming at peaceful
protesters. it appears, it is harder for a cop to mistake a flyswatter

for a racket than it is to mistake a hairbrush for a gun. before a wall,
built by bodies, the cyborg stands. fists the sky. the crowd chants

for freedom; for a day, faithful enough to let love blossom. in the video,
the cyborg is seen seething through scrums of bullets. there's a version

that ends where the cyborg feeds death to its own end & elsewhere,
a woman sings the national anthem before burning our country's flag.

News Reports Confirm the Cyborg is Missing

walking out of the *masjid*, i'm asked if i still desire
to be the wound that outpaces
the healing hands of time.

a man hands me a newspaper with a headline:
SINCE 2012, AS MANY AS 2000 WOMEN
HAVE BEEN HELD CAPTIVE BY BOKO HARAM.

in my room   a stray moth   flutters helplessly
around a lamplight   i watch my shadow tremble
across the windowless walls   police officers
stop by my house   to ask a few questions   i tell them
the cyborg & i played chess the night before   i offer them
cups of coffee   i tell them he loved the country
in a way i couldn't   when asked if anyone has
ever gone
lost in my family   i tell them we come from water
my grandfather had a crocodile   for an alter ego
i speak   with a faux conviction   my mouth—
a faucet
flooding the room with lies   i say nothing
about the women   who drown   seeking safety
in the maws of rivers   i tell them
the borg often choked   on the smoke
of our burning cities   they ask   if i'm shocked
by recent events in the country   i tell them
everyone i've lost   returns to me as wind
i excuse myself

to ululate in the bathroom   the sobbing—an offering
to quiet the memories   swelling in my chest
they ask   if the cyborg had any enemies
        i point to my country   on an atlas

The Cyborg Asks for My Excuses

i thought staying quiet was enough   i didn't know
the men in balaclavas were armed   i was trying
to stop a fly from licking blood off a wound on the
neck of a dead girl   i had no idea that women
were jumping into rivers   to escape gunmen
i needed more time   with the lost boy i found
on an empty playground   i was far away from
home   i heard the gunshots
but never asked which body they sought   if only
i'd listened to the radio that morning   i didn't
remember
it was some people's reality   when i captured
all the pieces on my chessboard   no part of me
thought it important to   report the lifeless
body i ran into   lying on a tarmac   it was too late
to save anyone   when i called the police   i wanted
to pull prayers from the Qur'an   to keep us
all safe   i was waiting for the smoke to clear out
i was busy   uploading names of missing people
into my memory bank   i felt i needed to record
videos of the plane
drawing arcs on the cloudless sky
i shouldn't have slept   with my headphones on

In Defense of Burnt Cities

as seen from the sky   the smoke never leaves
it opens a window   in memory & builds itself
a home   in all fairness   i shouldn't have asked
why the woman   threw her necklaces inside
the backseat of a burning car   i hadn't realized
that by tracing the map of the country   i was
attempting to wipe the ashes of burnt cities
i knew there'd been   missing women who were
unreported in the media   perhaps the rivers
needed someone to remind them that   they could
put out the fire   i guess   no one thought
the smoke meant something was learning
to become ash   firefighters must have grown
to believe running through smoke was a sport
for the city dwellers   i might have to give new
names to buildings with charred walls   it is now
pointless to ask   where the first fire came from
the answer is in the ashes   the answer
is in the eyes of the girl   with a pocketful of []

Leaked Footage of the Cyborg in an Interrogation Room

sitting under the interrogation lamp   the cyborg
draws clusters of imaginary circles on the table
i watch half the bright light wash over his face
what's left of it   sneaks through a half-silvered
mirror   into the darkened eyes of the detective
& in this moment   those who've left their homes
for cities outside the country   know nothing
about the arrests   or the many ways their houses
are now being folded in shrouds of silence
back in my hometown   boats are being paddled
on cinnamon-colored rivers   while police patrol
for tongues   accused of leaking intel to insurgents
in the footage   the detective presses the cyborg
for names of unknown gunmen   & the hands
that taught the townswomen to run toward rivers
each time a bullet begs to own their breaths
when asked who fired the first shot
into the crowd   during a protest   the cyborg drags
his left foot on the floor   & that too   is a prayer
for every demise he has witnessed   while i watch
the footage   outside my room   boys in threadbare
jean jackets   share stories of the cities they passed
before arriving here   my hometown's memory
unfolds in my mind   it returns to me as halos
of snow   farmlands   stained green by pastures
the beaten glimmer of zinc rooftops   darkened
by rust   the air   swollen with the laughter

of children on playgrounds   in the footage
the cyborg mutters a prayer he learned
from the Qur'an   his face glows   pale as street-
lights on a moonless night

While a Newly Elected President Is Being Sworn In

i watch campaign posters
get ripped from walls.
a car tire is set on fire
in the middle of a road.
on the phone, my sister
tells me to stay indoors.
until quietude returns.
her voice, treading behind
her series of anxiety attacks.
i burn a hole into
the arm of my couch.
i watch the smoke swirl
around the room like
a lost child. i fall asleep
on the floor. i dream of
a world where no one lives
to know what a bullet leaves
behind when it's pulled
out of a body. i yearn
for a day emptied of noise.
online, a girl sends me
photographs of towns,
invaded by bandits
before the elections. i think

about the days where i feel
myself floating like a leaf
above water. & others, where
i feel like a hairpin on an ocean
floor, waiting patiently for rust.

REACHING AN ENDPOINT

as it has done at the end of every storm
the city, like a caterpillar crawling out of
its shell, opens itself again, to a new quiet
skylight spreads on the people's aged darkness
rising from the ruins, everyone goes their way
each with a wound to nurse
a handful of memories blotted by blood
the men return to their workplace
the women go back to wearing loose-fitting
dresses. an army truck galumphs past elders
trudging the skin of prayer beads on a veranda.
back in their now almost roofless house, a girl
asks her mother if they've reached the point
in their suffering where they can say they've
survived. elsewhere, a boy on a playground
picks a wedding ring—*together forever*, carved
into its body. skimming through the footages
on a camera, i watch a man trace the edges
of a tombstone with a broken arm. his face
a broken beam easing into the arms of
darkness. the camera's eye closes & mine open
to the memories carving daylight into my sleep.

After a Conversation about Janazah
with Bhabi in a Dream

i wake drunk on the smell of my kufi liquefying under sunlight.
i touch the sea under my eyes hoping to pick wishbones from its bed.

i watch a cat fight for its life as it gulps mouthfuls of mud water in a pond
& i do not know if i want to save it or drown with it. therapy:

find an orifice in language & give your trauma a home.
i'm trying hard not to say i'm finding myself in every dirge on the internet

but man, these things kinda look so much like me. but we are fucking good,
right? i mean, if i keep my head down, go on about writing poetry on the leaflets

of my sedatives & nurse every bruise i pick from falls while sleepwalking
out of my nightmares, right? i must say though, my God, fuck these nightmares.

here i am, feeling alive, undead as tomorrow. here i am, watching as the night
rolls out to shroud the light in my room. fear grows on my tongue, i mistake it

for my language. darkness coalesces into an epitaph. i wait
until the night pours itself into a glass of water on the table & the table spreads out

like a river. the river is without a tributary—it opens & closes
in the eyes of a boy. the boy floats with flowers in his mouth. mouth here

is my country where a father stands before his son's body during janazah
& no one cries 'cause he lived like a nightingale with elegies for birdsongs.

lord, guide my father's hands to press the coma out of my breastbone should
   i ever oversleep

& slip towards the edge of death—& this better not be yet another
   unanswerable prayer.

Uncensored Footage of the
Cyborg at the U.S. Embassy

when he's stopped by security guards for a strip search,
i move my eyes away from the screen. i face the magazine
sitting on my table. i turn the radio on. i hear a woman
ask for donations to pay off the ransom for her kidnapped
husband. i pour myself a glass of cow milk. i sweep pieces
off a chessboard with my palm. i turn the tv on. a presenter
interrupts a program to break the news of migrants
found dead on the coast of river niger. i look down
the streets through my window. i take my gaze away
when i see a man being chased by police officers. i make excuses
for my disinterest in the country's ache. i pretend not
to notice when the cyborg kneels in front of a bomb detector.
i scroll through my twitter feed. outside my room, i hear
women returning from a wake, tell an officer
they're out to fulfill their duty of escorting the dead
with prayers, to their new home. in the footage, i watch
the cyborg walk into a room. his hands flying imaginary
planes in the air. he stops in front of a painting
of the white house, hanging on a wall. an american
woman asks what he came looking for at the embassy.
what he knows of american history. how long he plans
to stay on the american soil. why he's decided to leave
nigeria at a time it needs people the most. does he
understand what it means to be unloved by a country
he calls home. the cyborg walks out of the room, throbbing
like a moth flying headfirst into a whirlwind of terror.

SURVIVOR'S GIFT

a garden of irises now grows where my family's
favorite shopping mall used to be.

in the end, i learn, even time
surrenders itself to memory.

in my dreams, i watch women who raised me pack
faded family photographs into emptied pillowcases.

like shadows, children trail blindly behind parents
on the road to refugee camps outside the country.

a woman uses my face to trace in her memory
what my mother looked like as a young girl

long before the first gunshot went off
in the middle of the city.

another blows prayers into her son's face,
before he leaves for school.

on the news, terrorists threaten to start killing
kidnapped train passengers.

elementary school teachers protest with placards
for unpaid salaries. cameroonian government

complain of a surge of asylum seekers
most of which are from my country. during visits,

i hear victims of bomb attacks on hospital beds,
empty endless rivers of curses into the deafened ears

of the government. hundreds of exiles get lost
in the sands, trying to cross the sahara desert.

after the stitches are removed, a boy stares
into a mirror at a face he fails to recollect

as his own. in a documentary, doctors struggle
to hold back the blood jetting through

a splintered vein in a girl's neck. on the cityscape
a dark cloud spreads silently like a tumor under an eye.

ESTRANGEMENT THEORY

no migrant knew how to prepare to move out
of the city   there's never enough time to
properly pack everything   sometimes   the only
thing left behind is a favorite dress   sometimes
a tribe   mostly a language   i watch a group
of girls get interviewed by unicef   from
their accents   i know the language their tongues
have lost   i can tell what the night
means to them   by hearing how they talk
about starless skies & what burns beneath them
those who've left   will always think of the city
as a faceless shadow pulling itself away from
a blackened wall   i read a world map while
the national anthem blares from my radio
speakers   my love for the country   a black ink
disappearing on a whiteboard   i have no right
to question the water filling the footprints
of migrants on the shores of river niger   i have
seen the skylight shift   away from the cityscape
when what forced my people to flee returns
i pray i have enough flowers for our graves

TRANSLATION

i will be here when the wound disappears   i will learn
to say *home*   when asked what the scar on my ankle
means   someone will say my name in swahili
i'll be told it means   to be lost between borders
i'll listen to live reports on new refugees arriving at
minawao camp   the message   clear as white water—
the country's ache   a hungry wormhole   obsessed
with growth   i will call the rivers home   in front
of everyone   & not mean to drown   out of the need
to escape insurgents   in my mouth   i'll hold
faint memories of the city   in the shape of stories
i'll share with a woman i will lay in bed with
while moonlight spreads on our scars   through
the window   the night will arrive   hurrying to fill
our hearts   i'll not sleep in it   knowing there are villages
being burnt before its eyes   i will not speak
to the night   it wouldn't mean that i am angry
of course i am angry that more people will flee   & all
i will have   is a country no one will be able to call home

RE-SHOOTS

as if i'm yet to witness events   enough
to keep me awake for the rest of my life

clips on a camera drag me down
a memory lane   we've been here a lot
nothing it shows me is new   the stories
no different from those it has told me before
the incidents play out on rewind—

masked shooters speed out of a village
on reverse   driving back in to relaunch
their attacks   a bullet wound closes
to leave clear skin   corpses in a graveyard
crawl out to offer their presence
when a bomb goes off   amputees
on hospital beds regrow their limbs
to lose them in a train attack

the bloodied rivers turn clear again
turbaned men put their knives back
into their sheaths   before testing
their sharpness on the shoulders
of teenage boys   a man's broken arm
straightens back into shape   abducted women
return home to their families   untouched

i shut my eyes in search of ways to steer these
memories out through a laceration in my head

Midnight in Maiduguri

For A.J.

years after the insurgence   abduljalal
offers me an invitation to his hometown
in maiduguri   sometimes he tells me
stories of how the insurgents built
their army   some of the boys he grew
up on the same street with got recruited
before the dark days   they had been incapable
of harm   had hands
untouched by the coldness of death
the second time he invites me
for eid festival   he tells me it's now safe
the celebrations there marvelous
as moonlight in winter   we get to
ride on horses   dressed in long flowing
attires   our heads   wrapped in horned
turbans   trumpeters trailing behind us
while drummers drape the air
with ear-piercing music
& since nightfalls have stopped being
wet blankets   dragging the shadows
of the past into their homes   we will go
out to see the nightlife in town   enjoy
songs that helped them survive rays
of the black sun that rose before their eyes

REBIRTH

bhabi says you can tell a homeless bird
by how long it lingers in the sky   perhaps
i'm not the only one dying to sing to God
about burning cities   meet me here
where a sigh flattens   into a last breath
i'm twelve & learning nothing
about forgetting   my eyes cannot unsee
whatever the wind winds into them
from my window   the moon snakes
through faceless stars until there's nothing dark
left of the sky to shovel into my eyes
the muezzin's voice calls my bones to prayers
what again   does it mean to sleep
today   i know nothing of forgetting
history will be here to kiss me into dawn
& i won't forget to leave my tongue
in its mouth   take this from me
memories of a burning homeland
cannot be washed by all the water
on earth   forgive me—my mother tongue
has no words to name this fire   eating
its flesh   but tonight   let's call it rebirth
& share a room in the body of the same God

DRONECODE

before flight, always put on a fake bullet-proof vest.
if you meet a crowd of mourners,
pretend no one is allowed to die in the country.
        when asked where you're flying to,
point to an invincible window
                hovering in airspace.
practice watching a water skater break through
the angle of incidence of sunlight on a pond.
when your drone complains of hunger,
                        feed it slivers of radium.
if police ask if it has a missile stuffed in its nose,
pull out rubber cement from your mouth.
        when someone asks about your privacy policy,
project a video of the president breakdancing in his bedroom.
        at a mass funeral, tell no one your drone
    can lead the dead into heaven's gates.
            when flying at night,
never expect dinosaurs to fall out of the sky.
if your drone pretends to land on an imaginary skyscraper,
                    name it the backbone of the earth.
never fly above a country trying to learn the art of war.
if your drone fractures its rotor blades,
        lift yourself skywards at a full throttle.
after buzzing through a sandstorm,
ask your drone if it'd like to land on the Atlantic
        for lubrication.
when asked if your drone can heal the world,
    press your ear to a tree and wait for God to answer.

CYBORG'S DIARY

I was told the insurgents, ██████████, will
return the abducted girls. President, ██████
██████ said he had everything in control.
The morning after, over forty farmers were killed
by ██████████, their bodies, found between
rows of ridges. Watching the morning news,
I learned some houses in town were becoming
emptier than whitespaces. For days, I wrote
letters to ██████
reminding them of the wound their silence was
opening. In ██, I met a woman named
██████ who wouldn't stop speaking to me
about a bloodied river flooding the hems of her
town. In that time, I was unconcerned with the
work of memory. I was worried someone would
ask about the screws on my elbows. Everyone
seemed too busy contemplating the radius of
exit wounds. ██ told me this meant survival
was close. When I arrived in a small village in
██████████, ██ was missing. ██ had been
arrested by police. ██ & his family were on
their way to a refugee camp in ██████████.
No one knew where ██████ had disappeared
to. It wasn't enough to keep ████'s name in
supplications. There had to be a way to bring
██ back home. In the middle of the year,
I traveled to ██████ for a meeting with ████
██. The air smelled of sweat. I drank so much

water. After I left, a suicide bomber was found in
█████'s courtyard. While buildings burned in
█████, I busied myself attending funeral prayers
of victims of a bomb attack by █████ in █████.
Returning to █████,
I slept on a bare floor, like a lost ring on a riverbed.

POST-MASSACRE PSYCH EVALUATION

I know what I've seen of blood & death—what the night forgets
to cover in its shadows; what part of paradise a bullet
undresses before the body, before stealing light from its eyes.

What was asked is, *are you healing or still hurting?*

I don't know what you're looking for in me
but in my sleep, I keep talking to dead bodies.
They speak back with a tongue the government hates;
with their mouthfuls of hurt—black holes, dying to swallow
the country that sashayed their souls to heaven.

How much did they pay for your silence?

Should the head be cut off from the body,
in fear of what this city of smoke & blood has to tell it?
I do not have all the answers. I know nothing of standing
for what's right. I'm scared of telling the truth.
There are shooters outside my window.

Why is this scar on your chin shaped like your country?

The dead wish we could hear what they say.
I can no longer speak of my needs on the street.
How do you translate this kind of silence?
There's a lot I cannot tell you. Nobody knows
the price of silence but all my friends are

traumatized or waiting for the sun to name
a part of them skidding towards oblivion.

On a scale of zero to God, please do something,
how much hope have you lost in life since the massacre?

I watch the police hose down the face of a man
with bullets. I watch the man fall like a dry leaf
in autumn. I watch the ground catch his blood
like raindrops. I watch his body slip into stillness.
Into God's silence. Into my sleep. Into my dreams.
I look up to the sky to watch God watching us in silence.

Do you feel tachyarrhythmia, shortness of breath, pressure
in the chest, tremors & hand sweating when you're stopped
by the police?

My sisters are afraid another man will be shot
for walking with his head up. I'm afraid I'll be buried
without my voice. My voice, my voice.
Did anyone hear my voice ask the government to end
police brutality? My God, my God, please do something
before they come for me.

DIRECTOR'S CUT
Recovered Footages from the Cyborg's Disk Drive

a woman wraps a bullet wound on her leg with a handkerchief.
naval officers pull drowned migrants by the wrist from a river.
a man in a prison cell asks his shadow why he has stitches on his arm.

police burn posters of women missing in the city.
vigilantes announce the arrival of gunmen on megaphones.
a child soldier's boots rusts by the foot of a watchtower.

tv houses broadcast the rise of abductions in the city.
exiles jump off a ship on its way back to the country.
taped escapees from a train attack quiver on a courtyard.

photographers take shots of buildings burning in the city.
protesters fall to their faces as tear gas clouds their eyes.
villagers dive into rivers to escape being shot by invaders.

a journalist lies dead with a bullet hole in her breast pocket.
returnees from refugee camps ask to live outside the city.
foreign tourists record videos of rivers reddened by blood.

in a speech, the president promises peace in the country.

reCAPTCHA Asks the Cyborg to Confirm He's Not a Robot

so i return the passport to its purse   perhaps
when next i try to leave   immigration officers
would have learned to look
beyond the snapped thread of scar on my jawline
i know i wear the face of everyone i share my blood
with   i need no reminding that where others find
healing   my hurt shudders into life   everyone i've loved
has left through water or death   so what makes me
different then   in my head   i've reached the part
where i forget what the flame takes with it
when a city burns   the part where nobody mistakes
my opened mouth for a frameless door to a scarred
country   the part where questions (about my name
my lineage   my origin   my people   my loss   my ideas
of home   my memories   & their dog-eared edges
my search for missing bodies   my love   & the rivers
i poured it into for my people) do not get to me
the part where i waste hours on end   sitting on the couch
while the tv plays soundlessly
& in the half-light of his room   the cyborg's eyes
skitters across a computer screen   he knows
what becomes of burning cities   once the smoke
clears out   so he searches his memory for songs
he learned from women in refugee camps
with palms   lifted toward heaven   he sings
on loop   he forgets the lyric that opens
the prayer   where the women said the passwords

are hidden   he paces through piles of papers
on the floor   on my couch i remind myself
to keep my eyes on the girl drifting on the dark
rivers of my memories   through a hole
in my window shutters   i watch a boy throw
burning boxes of wool over barricades
at a checkpoint   i teach myself to be a blind witness
                        before police arrive

After Escaping Fire

Do you remember anything?
i watched in silence, how insignias of wars tumbled
off their tongues when they opened their mouths
to speak. the country's name carried like a curse
by our fathers & their fathers, got torn to shreds.
Do you remember anything more important than this?
hills of smoke branching out of houses.
warcrafts, sieving the chaffs of serenity
left in our bodies. a bullet, or more, looking for a home
in my father's chest; in between my mother's breasts.

Where were you?
the edge of a city. learning to build
a home out of fire; out of ashes, left
by my brothers' bodies, on our playground.

What did they say?

...

Are you even listening? What did they say?
gunshots. explosions. fire.
we bring you peace; as-salaam alaikum.

What did they take?
what we thought even the wind had
no hands to touch in our bodies.

What did they leave?
children, sleeping in bedrooms
that turn graveyards in the morning.

How do you sleep?
crouched beside the undying memories of:
homes, twirling to the echoes of gunshots;

men, bathing the country with the blood of her children;
bullets sneaking into the spines of families & not leaving;
generations of future leaders fed to hands that open
the mouth of fire; with my eyes opened.

How do you sleep?

HOMECOMING

it must mean a lot to the world
that you no longer have any memory of it.
that you do not remember picking up the phone
to be told that your father has forgotten his way
back home again. that he's probably out there
naked, shooting at imaginary enemies in a war
that has been over for over a hundred years—
before colonization, national flags, & anthems.
it must mean a lot to the world
that i am holding you in my arms, & you are not
trailing off into the dark corners of another memory.
that my hands reach for yours & i am not met
with blood. that on the floor where we lay,
our bodies, simmering in sweat, i read to you
about birds & flight. to keep them both alive
you let a sky unfold from the alleys of your palms
for the first time in years since he left you & your
mother, to fight out of love for his country;
since he returned with the silencer of a 9mm pistol
dangling like a cigar, from his mouth; with stories where
every character dies with a bullet between their eyes
& he, the teller, blames it on the quiet of his audience.

EVENSONG

standing under a straw of moonlight
falling through a hole in the roof
your body is bending in that way again
where light pours from it in billows
i'm begging your shadow on the wall
to be carried under your wing   i know how
in your arms   the universe
& its weight on my shoulders   withers
somewhere   a woman is being taught
to whisper one of the ninety-nine names of Allah
into her palms to attenuate her grief
the last time a smile pressed itself
against her cheekbone   there wasn't enough
water in her bones to drown a memory
in minna   a man lost his wife
in a fire outbreak & hasn't stopped
searching for her face in every smoke
cradling the sky   now that i'm here
picking whorls of silence off your tongue
i'm nosing out the vocabulary of your [un?]happiness
like sunset caressing the quietude of water
the grammar is blindly beautiful   this is where
i'm dying to delve into your smile   to drown in your mirth
Lord, please, please, answer my

CAST (In Order of Disappearance)

blue-skies—
wiped out of sight
by a giant surf of smoke
while everyone watched
with arms raised toward
heaven, at the raging flames
ushering a black sun into town.

    quietude—
    chased out of town
    by the chatter of firearms.

genealogy—
waited until nightfall
before drifting into the
darkened rivers whose
mouths close outside
the country.

    cyborg—
    tired of tending
    to the wounds in my
    stories, flew back to space.

widowed women—
ran through large banners

storekeepers—
ran through the streets
screaming the shahada
with the dried air in their
lungs. begging Allah to make
their bodies invincible to the
peeled eyes of bullets.

schoolchildren—
taken in their uniforms
into a skyless forest.

the woman i am in love with—
promised to write me every week
when her family finds a safe place
abroad. i burn her
favorite incense sticks every night
hoping the smoke leads me to her.

bhabi—
tired of carrying the lives
of the many women in my life,
left with my love leaking from her heart.

security officers—
left their stations

of smoke
after the escalation
of violence in the town.

school teachers—
stopped showing up
when no one in the country
could claim the burnt girl's body.

for the riverside
to wash away every memory of
bullet holes making home of bodies.

townspeople—
crouched in marshes
waiting for the gunfire
to return silence to their homes.

NOTES AND SOURCE ACKNOWLEDGMENTS

The title "my god swears / by the fig, by the olive, by the brightest star, by the prophet who penned no ghazal" is taken from Sarah Ghazal Ali's "Ghazal Ghazal." "WORMHOLE," "DRONECODE" and "APOCALYPSE" are written after Sinead Overbye, Samyak Shertok, and Franny Choi, respectively.

Grateful acknowledgment to the editoers and staff of the publications in which some of these poems were previously published (sometimes in earlier forms or under different titles):

Agbowo: "APOCALYPSE"

Black Cat Magazine: "6pm at AbdulHameed's Barbershop"

Boston Review: "The BBC Explains the Country's Challenges to the Cyborg in 60 seconds" and "Uncensored Footage of the Cyborg at the US Embassy"

carte blanche: "ROAD MAP" and "AURORA"

Covert Literary Magazine: "DRONECODE"

FIYAH: "Explaining Bots Fight to Bhabi"

International Human Rights Arts Festival: "Uncensored Footage of the Cyborg Leading a Protest in Lagos"

Iskanchi Press & Magazine: "Evensong" and "Everything I've Lost Returns to me as Wind"

Lolwe: "MAQTOOB," "RHUBARB SHOT" and "Midnight in Maiduguri"

Mizna: "News Reports Confirm the Cyborg is Missing," "A Patrol Officer wants to know," and "Wreckville"

Palette Poetry: "Ars Poetica with a Broken Shahada"

Rockvale Review: "After Escaping Fire"

So To Speak Journal: "Introducing Bhabi to the Cyborg"

The Drinking Gourd: "my god swears / by the fig, by the olive, by the brightest star, by the prophet who penned no ghazal"

Uncanny Magazine: "WORMHOLE," "POST MASSACRE PSYCH EVALUATION," and "DRIVING DOWNTOWN"

Zone 3 Press Magazine: "REBIRTH" and "HOMECOMING"

*Seven New Generation African
Poets: A Chapbook Box Set*
Edited by Kwame Dawes
and Chris Abani
(Slapering Hol)

*New-Generation African Poets:
A Chapbook Box Set (Tano)*
Edited by Kwame Dawes
and Chris Abani
(Akashic Books)

*Eight New-Generation African
Poets: A Chapbook Box Set*
Edited by Kwame Dawes
and Chris Abani
(Akashic Books)

*New-Generation African Poets:
A Chapbook Box Set (Sita)*
Edited by Kwame Dawes
and Chris Abani
(Akashic Books)

*New-Generation African Poets:
A Chapbook Box Set (Tatu)*
Edited by Kwame Dawes
and Chris Abani
(Akashic Books)

*New-Generation African Poets:
A Chapbook Box Set (Saba)*
Edited by Kwame Dawes
and Chris Abani
(Akashic Books)

*New-Generation African Poets:
A Chapbook Box Set (Nne)*
Edited by Kwame Dawes
and Chris Abani
(Akashic Books)

*New-Generation African Poets:
A Chapbook Box Set (Nane)*
Edited by Kwame Dawes
and Chris Abani
(Akashic Books)

To order or obtain more information on these or other University of
Nebraska Press titles, visit nebraskapress.unl.edu. For more information
about the African Poetry Book Series, visit africanpoetrybf.unl.edu.